HANUMAN CHALISA FOR KIDS

Rahul Agrawal & Arjun Agrawal

NOTE TO PARENTS

As far as I can remember I have been singing Hanuman Chalisa since I was around 10 years old. It all started with competition among cousins on who could sing the most verses. It did not matter to us that we barely understood the meaning of most of it.

Fast forward 30 years and I wanted my six year old boy, Arjun to sing and learn Hanuman Chalisa as well. We have been living outside India for some time and all the stories of Ramayan, Mahabharat and Dashavtar seemed a good medium to keep him connected to our roots and also explain the cultural significance of a civilization which goes back tens of thousands of years.

I had to make Hanuman Chalisa interesting for Arjun or else he would have lost interest. Thus, I started narrating each line to him every night and explain the stories and meaning behind each one of them. Afterwards, I started writing one verse at a time on a whiteboard and explain the meaning of each word and line to him. We also discussed stories and lessons from each verse. Arjun immediately developed a liking for it and found this very interesting. What started as a simple exercise to make Arjun learn Hanuman Chalisa finally manifested as this book.

The fact that you have bought this book for your little one says that we share the same thoughts and values. I sincerely hope that this book meets your expectations and is a step forward in the direction to teach your little one about Hanumanji. I also hope that this book will provide you an opportunity to share some quality time together with your child and discuss the glories of Sri Ramchandra and Hanumanji together. Start with one verse at a time and see the magic of Hanumanji come to life in your child.

Jai Sri Ram.

This book is dedicated to our original Super Hero

HANUMANJI

काज किये बड़ देवन के तुम बीर महाप्रभु देखि बिचारो ।
कौन सो संकट मोर गरीब को जो तुमसो नहिं जात है टारो ।।

You have done so many deeds for Gods. O Brave Lord (Hanumanji), just give it a thought.
Which problem of mine, a poor soul, cannot be resolved with a glance of yours.

Hanuman Ashtak

Jai Sri Ram

जय श्री राम

Hanumanji is our original Superhero. Before there were Batman, Superman, Spiderman there was Hanuman. He was born as a vanara to Kesari and Anjana. They prayed to Lord Shiva for a child and were blessed with the divine child. Vayu, the wind God was instructed to carry Lord Shiva's divine magical power to Anjana.

Even as a child, Hanumanji had immense strength and courage. Once he leapt up in the sky to eat Sun thinking of it as a sweet fruit. All the Gods had to intervene and then Lord Indra blessed him with supreme powers. He played a key role in Ramayana and helped Sri Ram look for Mata Sita and fight Ravan in the war of Lanka.

Hanumanji had powers to fly, to change himself into either a tiny or a gigantic form, lift a mountain and many more. At the same time, he was also very humble, wise and intelligent. He was always ready to help others and had complete selfless devotion towards Sri Ram.

All of this has been very beautifully described by Tulsidasji in Hanuman Chalisa, the glories of Hanumanji in forty verses. Even after almost 400 years of Hanuman Chalisa, it is one of the most famous prayers chanted daily by millions of Hindus around the world.

Jai Sri Ram. जय श्री राम ।

श्री हनुमान चालीसा

TEACHER   FEET   LOTUS   DUST   SELF   MIND   MIRROR   CLEAN

श्री गुरु चरन सरोज रज निज मन मुकुर सुधारि।
बरनौ रघुवर बिमल जसु जो दायकु फल चारि॥

NARRATE   FROM RAGHU CLAN SRI RAM   PURE   GLORIOUS   WHICH   GIVES   FRUIT   FOUR

shree guru charan saroj raj nij man mukur sudhari|
barnou raghuvar bimal jasu jo dayak phal chari||

With the dust of lotus feet of Teacher / By touching the feet of my Guru, I clean the mirror of my mind

I narrate the glorious story of Raghuvar who gives the four fruits of life

Hanuman Chalisa is composed of forty verses and has two doha (दोहा) at the beginning and one at the end.

In the very first doha here, Tulsidasji pays respect to his Guru (teacher) by touching his feet. Tulsidasji requests the blessings of his teacher so that he can clear his mind and focus on writing the glories of Sri Ram and Hanumanji.

The four fruits mentioned here are Dharma (धर्म), Artha (अर्थ), Kama (काम) and Moksha (मोक्ष). These Sanskrit words do not have English translation but can be referred as Moral Values (dharma), Prosperity (artha), Pleasures (kama) and Liberation (moksha).

These four virtues are also called objectives (अर्थ) of human (पुरुष) life or Purusartha (पुरुषार्थ).

श्री हनुमान चालीसा

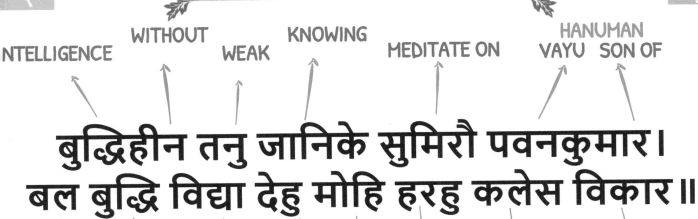

INTELLIGENCE · WITHOUT · WEAK · KNOWING · MEDITATE ON · HANUMAN VAYU · SON OF

बुद्धिहीन तनु जानिके सुमिरौ पवनकुमार।
बल बुद्धि विद्या देहु मोहि हरहु कलेस विकार॥

STRENGTH · WISDOM · KNOWLEDGE · GIVE ME · REMOVE · AILMENTS · IMPURITIES

budhhi heen tanu janike sumiro pavankumar|
bal budhi vidya dehu mohi harhu kalesh vikar||

Knowing myself as ignorant, I meditate on Pavan Kumar (Hanumanji)
Give me strength, wisdom and knowledge and remove all my ailments
and impurities

Tulsidasji knows that writing the glory of Sri Ram is not an easy task. In the previous line, he first requests the blessings of his teacher. In this line, he acknowledges himself as ignorant to take on this difficult task. Therefore he first prays to Hanumanji and requests his blessings for strength, wisdom and knowledge. With this he starts this journey of writing the glorious tales of Sri Ram and Hanumanji.

Tulsidasji knows that Hanumanji is the greatest devotee of Sri Ram. And when somebody prays to Hanumanji their prayer reaches Sri Ram as well. Therefore, he requests Hanumanji to remove his mind of any impurity or ailments. Next he writes forty lines in praise of Hanumanji, the Hanuman Chalisa.

VICTORY   HANUMAN   KNOWLEDGE   QUALITY WISDOM   OCEAN

जय हनुमान ज्ञान गुन सागर।
जय कपीस तिहुँ लोक उजागर॥

VICTORY   MONKEY   GOD   THREE   WORLD   BRIGHTEN

jai hanuman gyan gun sagar| jai kapeesh tihu lok ujaagar||

Victory to Hanuman, the ocean of knowledge and wisdom
Victory to the Greatest Vanara who is famous across three worlds
Or whose stories brighten the three worlds

Hanuman Chalisa is composed using choupai (चौपाई), a Hindi poetic style using four syllable verses.

In the very first choupai, Tulsidasji prays for victory to Hanumanji. He is not just very brave and mischievous but is also very knowledgeable and wise. He is the greatest vanara ever. Kapeesh literally means the Monkey King. Kapee (कपी) is Monkey and Eesh (ईश) is God or King, the greatest. As per Valimki Ramayana Vanara were forest dwelling humans with some features like monkey.

As per our ancient scriptures, there are 14 lokas. 7 upper and 7 lower with earth being the 7th one. Tulsidasji here simplifies this into three loka as Heaven (स्वर्ग), Earth (पृथ्वी) and Underworld (पाताल). In Hindu culture, we generally avoid using the word hell and we say Underworld or Paataal. There are creatures living below the earth or underworld who may be less evolved than creatures living on earth. Hanumanji's glory is famous across all these worlds.

SRI RAM — MESSENGER — UNCOMPARABLE A LOT — STRENGTH — HOLDER

राम दूत अतुलित बल धामा।
अंजनि पुत्र पवनसुत नामा॥

ANJANI (HANUMANJI'S MOTHER) — SON — WIND — SON — NAMED

ram doot atulit bal dhama| anjani putra pavansut nama||

You are Sri Ram's messenger and you have immense strength
You are Anjani's son, also known as Son of Wind God (Pavan)

Anjani or Añjanā was an apsara named Punjikastala. Due to a curse from Sage Durvasa, she was born as a vanara princess on earth. Later she married a vanara chief, Kesari and gave birth to Hanumanji. Therefore, Hanumanji is also called Anjani putra (अंजनि पुत्र).

Kesari and Anjani prayed to Shiva for a child. Shiva was very pleased by their prayers and granted them the boon. On his instruction, Vayu, the God of Wind, carried Shiva's divine power to Anjana's tummy and Hanumanji was born. Hanumanji is known by many names including Pavansut (पवनसुत) Son of Wind God, Maruti Nandan (मारुती नंदन) Son of Air God and Kesari Nandan (केसरी नंदन) Son of Kesari.

GREATEST HERO
GREAT BRAVE

HAVING
COURAGE

BODY AS STRONG AS
VAJRA – INDRA'S WEAPON

महावीर विक्रम बजरंगी।
कुमति निवार सुमति के संगी॥

BAD THOUGHTS   TAKES AWAY   GOOD THOUGHTS   COMPANION
WHO STAYS WITH YOU

mahaveer vikram bajrangi| kumati niwar sumati ke sangi||

You are the Greatest Hero, courageous and your body is strong as Vajra
You are the destroyer of Bad Qualities/Intellect/Thoughts
You are Companion of People with Good Qualities/Intellect/Thoughts

Su (सु) – in Hindi is generally used for something good and Ku (कु) – for bad.
e.g. Suputra – Good Child and Kuputra – Bad Child

Tulsidasji here invokes us to seek the company of friends with positive thoughts and behaviour. He asks us to stay away from the ones with evil thoughts and action.

Once Bal Hanuman leapt in the sky to eat Sun thinking of it as a sweet fruit. All the Gods were scared and requested Indra for help. Indra hurled his vajra (thunderbolt) on Hanuman. This angered Vayu and he sucked all air from atmosphere. Indra then revived the unconscious chid and gave boon to Hanumanji that his body will be as strong as his Vajra (वज्र). Anga (अंग) means Body. Thus Bajrangi means someone whose body is as strong as Indra's Vajra.

GOLDEN COMPLEXION COLOR SHINING WELL DRESSED GOOD LOOKS

कंचन बरन बिराज सुबेसा।
कानन कुंडल कुंचित केसा॥

EAR ROUND EARRING CURLY HAIR

kanchan baran beeraj subesha | kaanan kundal kunchit kesa ||

You look beautiful with golden hue and you shine in your beautiful attire

You wear round earrings on your ears and you have curly hair

This line describes how Hanumanji looks. Even though Hanumanji has the appearance of a monkey, he is described so beautifully here by Tulsidasji.

As per one legend, Vali the vanara king came to know of a divine child being born to Anjani. He made a dart of five metals and aimed at Anjani. However, because of Hanumanji's divine power nothing happened to him and he was born with a pair of beautiful earrings.

Hanumanji's natural complexion is of golden hue. But we also see him in red color.

This is a very beautiful story. Once Hanumanji saw Mata Sita applying red sindoor (vermillion) on her forehead. He asked her about it but Mata Sita could not find an appropriate answer and said "It is for the longer life of Prabhu Sri Ram". Then Hanumanji thought if a small dot can increase Sri Ram's life then I will apply it all over my body for even longer life of my Prabhu.

HAND   VAJRA   AND   FLAG   HAVE / RESTS

हाथ बज्र औ ध्वजा बिराजै।
काँधे मूँज जनेऊ साजै॥

SHOULDER   TYPE OF GRASS   SACRED THREAD   DECORATES

haath bajra au dhwaja beeraje | kaandhe moonj janeu saaje ||

You carry Bajra (Indra's weapon) in one hand and flag on other hand
The sacred thread (janeu) made of munj grass decorates your
shoulder

The first line here can be interpreted in a variety of ways. Although the line says that Hanumanji is carrying Vajra in his hand, we generally see Hanumanji carry a mace (गदा).
It can also mean that his hands are as strong as Vajra and he is carrying the flag of victory on the other hand.

Janeu (जनेऊ) represents a sacred thread which was typically given to young students o acceptance to Gurukul in a ceremony called Upanayan. Wearing a janeu was considered very important stage of life and signified coming of age. This was generally carried on before the age of twelve and meant childhood was over and the time had come to attain formal education The person wearing Janeu has the responsibilit to exercise self-control and attain knowledge.

shankar suvan kesari nandan| tej pratap maha jag bandan||

You are Shiva (Shankar's) avatar son of Kesari (vanara chief)
Your aura and glory is so great that the whole world worship you

When Vishnu took the avatar of Ram, Shiva (also known as Shankar) also incarnated on earth as Hanumanji to help and serve Sri Ram. Shiva took the form of monkey so that he can serve his master, Sri Ram.

It is really interesting in stories that both Sri Ram and Shiva love and respect each other and can also be seen praying to each other.

Kesari was a vanara king. He was Hanumanji's father. Together with Anjana, Kesari prayed to wind god (Vayu) for a child. Vayu carried Shiva's divine power and they were blessed with Hanumanji.

Thus Hanumanji is referred as the incarnation of Shiva (शंकर) and son of Pavan (पवन) and Kesari (केसरी).

KNOWLEDGE INTELLIGENT GOOD QUALITIES A LOT CLEVER

विद्यावान गुनी अति चातुर।
राम काज करिबे को आतुर॥

SRI RAM WORK DO TO EAGER

vidyavaan gunee ati chaatur | ram kaaj karibe ko aatur ||

You are very intelligent and have lots of very good qualities. You are also very clever

You are also very eager to do anything for Sri Ram

The previous lines explained the strength and courage of Hanumanji.

This line explains that he is also very intelligent and humble. Even with so much power and wisdom he was always eager to do anything for Sri Ram. This line reminds us to learn humility from Hanumanji.

Doing any task for Sri Ram brought extreme joy and satisfaction to Hanumanjj.

He was the first one to volunteer to go look for Mata Sita, even though he had to cross a vast ocean with extreme difficulties. Remember this was a time when there were no maps or GPS, yet he went around searching for Sita not knowing what is on the other side of the vast ocean.

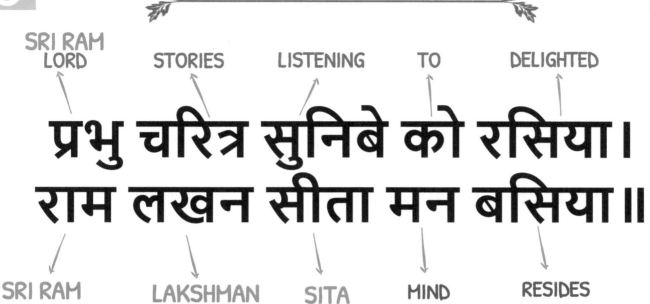

prabhu charitra sunibe ko rasiya| ram lakhan sita man basiya||

You get delighted listening to Lord Ram's (Prabhu) stories
Ram, Lakshman and Sita reside in your heart or
You live in the hearts of Ram, Lakshman and Sita

Hanumanji always gets delighted listening to stories and acts of Sri Ram. Prabhu Sri Ram is the gold standard of perfection. In our stories, Sri Ram is shown as the ultimate human being, the Maryada Purushottam (मर्यादा पुरुषोत्तम).
This line has a very deep meaning for us and inspires us to always be in the company of good people and read their stories and acts.

Hanumanji was once gifted a pearl necklace by Mata Sita. He bit every pearl and started throwing them away. When asked, he said that the pearls are of no value to him as it does not contain Sri Ram in it. When probed further he tore his chest to show the figures of Sri Ram and Mata Sita residing there.

TINY FORM ASSUME SITA SHOWN

सूक्ष्म रूप धरी सियहिं दिखावा।
बिकट रूप धरि लंक जरावा॥

MASSIVE FORM TAKE LANKA BURNT

sukshma roop dharee siyahi dikhava | bikat roop dhari lanka jarava ||

You took the tiny form and showed yourself to Sita
And you took the massive form and burnt down Lanka

When Hanumanji went to look for Mata Sita, he found her sitting under a tree at Ashok Vatika. She was very weak and sad. Hanumanji took the form of a tiny (सूक्ष्म रूप), childlike monkey and started singing "Sri Ram Jai Ram Jai Jai Ram". This caught Sitaji's attention and she felt genuine love and trust for this tiny creature.

At the same time when Hanumanji was presented before Ravan, the Lanka King, he made fun of Hanumanji's monkey looks and also insulted Sri Ram. Ravan even lighted his tail to teach him a lesson. Hanumanji then took massive form (बिकट रूप) and burnt the golden city of Lanka to break his arrogance.

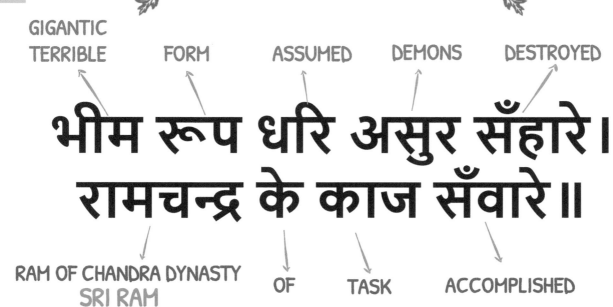

GIGANTIC TERRIBLE — FORM — ASSUMED — DEMONS — DESTROYED

भीम रूप धरि असुर सँहारे।
रामचन्द्र के काज सँवारे॥

RAM OF CHANDRA DYNASTY SRI RAM — OF — TASK — ACCOMPLISHED

bhima roop dhari asura sanhare| ramchandra ke kaaj sanware||

You took the gigantic form and destroyed all the demons
You accomplished/made easy all the task for Sri Ramchandra

Bhima (भीम) here means really big and gigantic and not Bhima from Mahabharat.
However, it is a really interesting use of Bhima in this line. Bhima is the also son of Vayu, the wind God as Hanumanji. Therefore, Hanumanji and Bhima are considered brothers.

We all know different stories of Hanumanji as part of Ramayana. But do you know Hanumanji appears prominently in the war of Mahabharat? Arjun's chariot carried the banner of Hanumanji during the Kurukshetra war.

BROUGHT   SANJEEVANI HERB   LAKSHMAN   SAVED LIFE

लाय सँजीवनि लखन जियाए।
श्रीरघुबीर हरषि उर लाए॥

BRAVE OF RAGHU DYNASTY SRI RAM   HAPPINESSS   HEART CLOSE   BROUGHT

laye sanjeevani lakhan jiyaye| shree raghubeer harshi ur laaye||

You brought Sanjeevani herb (booti) and saved Lakshman's life
And with this you brought joy and happiness to Sri Ram (Sri Raghuveer)

Lakshman was wounded in the war by Indrajit and fell unconscious. Then Hanumanji flew all the way to Himalayas to look for Sanjeevani herb. Although he found the mountain but could not identify the herb. Still he did not give and brought the whole mountain with him.

Vaidya (Doctor) Sushena then used the herb to revive Lakshman. Prabhu Sri Ram was extremely happy and joyful seeing Lakshman come back to life.
The line here teaches us that even if we face extreme difficulties in life we should not give up and look for ways to deal with the situation.

KING OF RAGHU DYNASTY
SRI RAM — DID — A LOT — PRAISE

रघुपति कीन्हीं बहुत बड़ाई।
तुम मम प्रिय भरतहि सम भाई॥

YOU — MY — DEAR — BHARAT — LIKE — BROTHER

raghupati keenhee bahut badai| tum mum priya bharathi sama bhai||

Sri Ram (Raghupati) praised you a lot (for getting Sanjeevani and saving Lakshman's life)

And said, "You are as dear to me as my brother Bharat"

All his brothers were very dear to Sri Ram. However, in this line, Tulsidasji makes a special mention of Bharat and Sri Ram equates Hanumanji with Bharat.

Bharat was the symbol of love and sacrifice. Even after getting the kingdom of Ayodhya he took Sri Ram's sandal (खड़ाऊ) and placed it on the throne making Sri Ram the actual King.

Sri Ram is also known as Raghupati or Raghav after his great grandfather Raghu (रघु) of Ikshvaku dynasty. Raghu was one of the greatest kings to rule over India.

Raghupati means the one who owns the land of Raghu and Raghav means scion of Raghu clan.

sahas badan tumharo jas gaaven| as kahi shreepati kanth lagaaven||

Thousands of people or the thousand headed serpent (Sheshnag)
sings your glory
Sri Ram (Sripati) embraced you after saying this

Seshnag is depicted as the thousand-headed serpent and Vishnu rests on him. Sheshnag took avatar as Lakshman along with Vishnu's avatar Sri Ram.

This is one of the many lines showing the poetic mastery of Tulsidasji where each line can be interpreted in a variety of ways. Here sahas badan (सहस बदन) can refer to both thousands of people and also Seshnag.

In this and previous lines, Tulsidasji shows the love and respect Sri Ram had for Hanumanji. When Hanumanji comes back from Lanka after searching for Mata Sita, Sri Ram gets overwhelmed and says there is nothing in this world which I can give to Thank you except my love and respect. He then embraces Hanumanji.

SANAK OTHERS (आदी) BRAHMA OTHERS MUNIS / RISHIS

सनकादिक ब्रह्मादि मुनीसा।
नारद सारद सहित अहीसा॥

NARAD SHAARAD (SARASWATI) INCLUDING AHEESA

sanaka-adik brahmadi munisa| naarad shaarad sahit ahisa ||

Saints and sages like Sanak, Gods including Brahma
Narad, Shaarad (Sarawati) and Aheesa (Serpent King) ..see next verse

In this and the next line, Tulsidasji explains that Hanumaji's glory is so great that even saints like Sanak, sages, Brahma, munis, Narad, Saraswati (Shaarad), Aheesa (Serpent King) combined cannot properly narrate his stories and glories.

Narad was a famous muni and great devotee of Vishnu. He used to travel across time and different worlds singing "Narayan Narayan" and narrating stories of Bhagwan. He was also called Devarshi or Dev Rishi.
Once he was cursed that although he would tell the truth and warn people about things to come, nobody will take him seriously.

YAM   KUBER   DIKPAL   WHERE   FROM

जम कुबेर दिक्पाल जहाँ ते।
कबी कोबिद कहि सकैं कहाँ ते॥

POETS   SCHOLARS FOLK SINGERS   SAY SING   ABLE   WHERE (?)

jam kuber dikpal jahaan te| kabi kobid kahi saken kahaan te||

Yam, Kuber, Dikpal (along with all the others mentioned in previous line)

And all poets and scholars together fail to sing your glory

Along with all the famous gods and rishi munis mentioned in the last line, even Yam (God of Death), Kuber (God of Wealth), Dikpal (God of Eight Directions), poets (कबी), scholars and folk singers (कोबिद) also fail to sing your endless glory.

Tulsidasji uses names from all three worlds (lokas) in these lines. Brahma and other gods residing in Swarga loka (Heaven), poets and scholars from Prithvi loka (Earth) and Aheesa (the serpent king) from the Patala loka (Underworld).

Therefore, everyone combined from three lokas are not able to sing the glories of Hanumanji.

YOU — FAVOR — SUGRIVA — DID

तुम उपकार सुग्रीवहिं कीन्हा।
राम मिलाय राजपद दीन्हा॥

SRI RAM — INTRODUCED — KINGDOM — GAVE

tum upkaar sugrivahin keenha | ram milaay rajpad deenha ||

You did a great favor on Sugriva

By introducing him to Sri Ram and got his kingdom back. (Ram helped Sugriva defeat Vaali and thus helped him get his kingdom back)

Sugriva and Vaali were brothers. However, Vali banished Sugriva from his kingdom at Kishkindha and Sugriva had to take refuge in the mountains. Once when Sugriva saw two princes walking towards the mountain, he sent Hanumanji to enquire about them.

Hanumanji disguised as Brahmin introduced himself to Sri Ram and sought his help to defeat Vaali. Sri Ram agreed to help Sugriva and ask Sugriva to invite Vaali for a fight challenge. Sri Ram shoots an arrow and kills Vaali, thus helping get Sugriva get his kingdom back.

YOUR   SUGGESTION   VIBHISHAN   ACCEPTED

तुम्हरो मन्त्र बिभीषन माना।
लंकेश्वर भए सब जग जाना॥

LANKA KING   BECAME   WHOLE   WORLD   KNOWS

tumharo mantra vibhishan mana| lankeshwar bhaye sab jag jaana॥

Vibhishan listened to your suggestion
And the whole world knows that he became the King of Lanka
afterwards

When Hanumanji reached Lanka, he went around searching all the palaces looking for Mata Sita. He came across a palace with a temple and newly planted Tulsi shrubs outside. He was really surprised to see this in Lanka, a town filled with gold and glitter. Hanumanji disguises himself as a sage and meets Ravan's brother Vibhishan at the palace. Vibhishan was elated to meet Sri Ram's messenger. Hanumanji then suggests Vibhishan to come to Sri Ram's refuge.

Later in Ravan's court, Vibhishan warns Rava for the abduction of Mata Sita. Ravan filled wit arrogance insults Vibhishan. He then leave Lanka to go to Sri Ram who was preparing fo battle with Ravan.

Vibhishan's insight about Lanka and it's arm proved really useful in the war and after Rava was defeated, Vibhishan was made king o Lanka (लंकेश्वर).

TIME DISTANCE → जुग
THOUSAND → सहस्र
DISTANCE (AROUND 12 KM) → जोजन
AT → पर
SUN → भानू।

TOOK → लील्यो
THAT → ताहि
SWEET → मधुर
FRUIT → फल
THINKING → जानू॥

juga sahastra jojan par bhaanu| lilyo taahi madhur phal jaanoo||

The Sun which is thousands of jojan (measure of distance) away
You took it thinking of a sweet fruit

Once when Hanumanji was a child he woke up feeling very hungry. He did not find Mother Anjana around. Just then Sun was rising and Hanumanji thought of it as a juicy yellow fruit. Being the son of Vayu he started flying towards the sun to eat this fruit. At that point, Sun got really scared and prayed to Indra to stop Bal Hanuman. Finally, Indra along with Vayu had to come to the rescue.

A Jojan (जोजन) is a measure of distance and is around 12 KM. Sahastra (सहस्र) is 1000 in number and Yuga is a calculation of years. Like many verses, even this line has a deep mystical meaning for us. It says that even though our goals may seem difficult in the beginning but with strong determination and effort we can achieve anything in life.

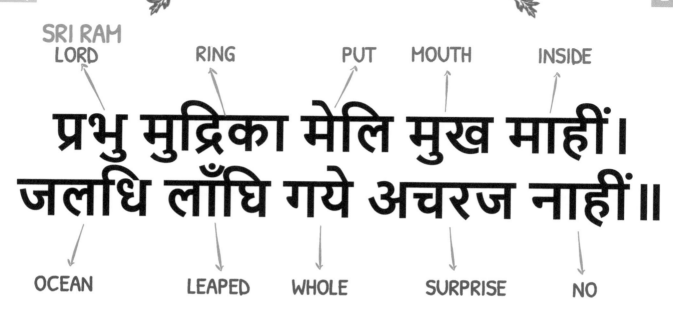

prabhu mudrika meli mukh maahee| jaladhi laanghi gaye acharaj naahi ||

You placed Sri Ram's ring in your mouth
And you leaped across the ocean, no surprise for you

When Hanumanji went around looking for Mata Sita, Sri Ram gave his ring (मुद्रिका) to Hanumanji so that he can show the ring to Mata Sita as a proof of him being Sri Ram's messenger.

Although, the line says Hanumanji placed the ring in his mouth it can also mean that Hanumanji had Sri Ram's name in his mouth (he kept chanting Sri Ram name) as he crossed the ocean to Lanka.

We have seen previously that even as a child Hanumanji flew in the sky to eat the sun thinking of it as a fruit. So, this time when he flew across the ocean to look for Mata Sita, it did not come as surprise to anyone.

The line here can also mean that each one of us has immense capabilities within us like Hanumanji. We just need to work hard to recognize it and find our true strength and then no task will be difficult for us.

श्री हनुमान चालीसा

DIFFICULT   TASK   WORLD   OF   ALTOGETHER

दुर्गम काज जगत के जेते । सुगम अनुग्रह तुम्हरे तेते॥

EASY   REQUEST GRACE   YOUR   THAT

durgam kaaj jagat ke jete | sugam anugrah tumhare tete ||

All the difficult tasks of the world
Becomes easy with your grace (When we pray to Hanumanji)

---

anuman Chalisa and the name of Hanuman has
agical powers for its true devotees.
one chants Hanuman Chalisa regularly and
rays to Hanumanji, all their difficult tasks start
become easier with the grace of Hanumanji
nd Sri Ram.

To achieve any goal in life we all have to work
really hard to earn it. Nothing comes in life
without hard work and devotion.
Tulsidasji asks us to not just work hard but also
have true devotion for Lord to achieve success
in life.

श्री हनुमान चालीसा

SRI RAM · COURT GATE · YOUR · PROTECTOR · WITHOUT · COMMAND · NO ONE · ENTER

राम दुआरे तुम रखवारे।
होत न आज्ञा बिनु पैसारे॥

ram duare tum rakhvaare | hota na aagya binu paisaare ||

You are the protector/gatekeeper to Sri Ram's court/abode
No one can enter Sri Ram's abode without your command/permission

The line says that Hanumanji is the gatekeeper to Sri Ram's court and nobody can enter there without his permission.

We can easily get to Sri Ram if we pray to Hanumanji and nothing better than chanting Hanuman Chalisa.

Ram Durbar (court) is a very common image in most Indian households with the image of Sri Ram in the center and Mata Sita and Lakshman on the two sides. Hanumanji is mostly seen kneeling with his hands folded.

श्री हनुमान चालीसा

ALL · PLEASURE · LIVE · YOUR · PLACE OF SHELTER

सब सुख लहै तुम्हारी शरना।
तुम रक्षक काहू को डरना॥

YOU · PROTECTOR · WHY · WORRY

sab sukh lahe tumhari sharna| tum rakshak kaahu ko darna ||

All pleasures are at your refuge / shelter
When you are the protector there is nothing to be afraid of

Tulsidasji asks us to go to Bhagwan's refuge and then Bhagwan will take care of you. When you go to someone's refuge and surrenders yourself then it becomes the other person's responsibility to take care of you.

Thus, if we surrender ourselves to Hanumanji then there is nothing to be worried about.

Goswami Tulsidasji was one of the greatest poets and saints. His most famous creation is Ramcharitmanas, a retelling of the original Ramayana in simple Awadhi, the language spoken in and around Ayodha.

The original Ramayana was composed in Sanskrit by Rishi Valmiki.

श्री हनुमान चालीसा

YOURSELF ENERGY CONTROL SELF

आपन तेज सम्हारो आपै।
तीनौं लोक हाँक ते काँपे॥

ALL THREE WORLD ROAR SHIVER

aapan tej samharo aape | teeno lok haank te kaanpe ||

You are the only one who can control your energy
The three world shiver with fear when you roar

As Hanumanji was son of Vayu and an avatar of Shiva, he had immense energy and supernatural powers. Tulsidasji here says that Hanumanji himself and nobody else can control this energy. And when Hanumanji roars with his full powers, everybody around the three world shivers with fear.

As a child, Hanumanji was very naughty. It was difficult to contain his energy and stay still. So, he went around playing tricks and disturbing sages and saints in their meditation. Once things got really out of hand and a rishi cursed Hanumanji that he will forget all his powers until someone reminds him of his powers at the right time. Later in Ramayana, Jambavan the bear king reminds Hanumanji of his immense powers and asks him to fly over the ocean to Lanka.

श्री हनुमान चालीसा

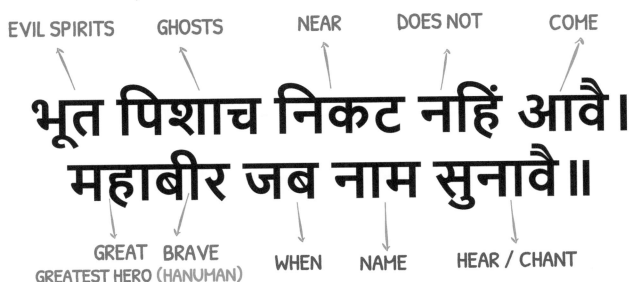

EVIL SPIRITS   GHOSTS   NEAR   DOES NOT   COME

भूत पिशाच निकट नहिं आवै।
महाबीर जब नाम सुनावै॥

GREAT BRAVE
GREATEST HERO (HANUMAN)   WHEN   NAME   HEAR / CHANT

bhoot pisaach nikat nahi aavei| mahaveer jab naam sunaave||

Evil spirits and ghosts do not come near
When they hear Hanuman's (Mahaveer) name or when one chants
Hanumanji's name

When you chant Hanuman Chalisa, it drives away all forms of evil spirits, ghosts and negative energies.
These negative energy can be both inside or outside us. Thus, taking Hanumanji's name purifies us from within as well.

This is one of the most popular lines of Hanuman Chalisa.
Children in India are taught this line and asked to repeat whenever they feel scared of anything. And Hanumanji will come to protect them.

श्री हनुमान चालीसा

DESTROYS SICKNESS TAKES AWAY ALL PAIN

नासै रोग हरै सब पीरा।
जपत निरंतर हनुमत बीरा॥

CHANT REGULAR HANUMAN BRAVE

nase rog hare sab peera | japat nirantar hanumat veera ||

You destroy all sickness and takes away all the pain
When someone takes / chants the name of brave Hanuman regularly

Like the previous line, this one also tells the magical powers of Hanuman Chalisa.
If you regularly chant Hanuman Chalisa, it frees you of all sickness, anxiety and pain.

Both a healthy mind and body are important for everyone.
Tulsidasji does not say that if we chant Hanuman Chalisa we will never be sick or there will be no pain, but Hanumanji gives us enough strength to fight us off any sickness and pain.
There is a famous saying "Pain is inevitable, but suffering is optional."

श्री हनुमान चालीसा

DIFFICULTIES OR CHALLENGES

FROM

HANUMAN

FREES

संकट तें हनुमान छुड़ावै।
मन क्रम बचन ध्यान जो लावै॥

MIND

ACTION

SPEECH

FOCUS CONCENTRATION

BRING

sankat te hanuman churave| man kram bachan dhyan jo laave||

Hanuman frees us from all difficulties/challenges
If we focus our mind, act and words on Him

Hanumanji is also commonly referred as (संकटमोचन) Sankat Mochan or "reliever of pain". If we bring our complete focus on Hanumanji including our mind, action and speech, he will relieve us of all difficulties and challenges.

There is a famous Sankat Mochan Hanuman Mandir in Varanasi on the banks of the Assi river. It is believed that Hanumanji once appeared before Tulsidasji. It is at this place Goswami Tulsidasji built a temple for Hanumanji.

ALL   SRI RAM   DISCIPLINED MEDITATING   KING

सब पर राम तपस्वी राजा।
तिन के काज सकल तुम साजा॥

WHOSE   TASK   ALL   YOU   EXECUTE

sab par ram tapasvee raja | tin ke kaaj sakal tum saja ||

Although, Sri Ram is the supreme king of all
But you still execute all his tasks (as caretaker)

Sri Ram is not just the King but also the Lord himself. However, when he incarnated on this earth as a mortal and faced challenges, Hanumanji executed a lot of tasks for him.

There are numerous examples of how Hanumanji helped Sri Ram including looking for Mata Sita, getting Sanjeevani herb to cure Lakshman and introducing him to Sugriva and Vibhishan. Such is the resourcefulness of Hanumanji.

A Tapasvee (तपस्वी) is like our ancient sages who used to lead a very disciplined life and were very skilled and knowledgeable men. Although they led a simple life, they were very resourceful and had lots of skills.

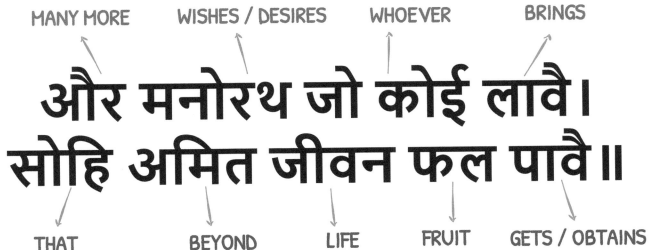

MANY MORE — WISHES / DESIRES — WHOEVER — BRINGS

और मनोरथ जो कोई लावै।
सोहि अमित जीवन फल पावै॥

THAT — BEYOND — LIFE — FRUIT — GETS / OBTAINS

aur manorath jo koi laave | sohi amit jeevan phal pave ||

And anyone comes to you with any wishes or desires
Their wishes are fulfilled beyond any limits (they get unlimited fruits)

We saw in the previous line that Hanumanji has immense capabilities to even help Sri Ram. Therefore, if we pray to Hanumanji he can fulfill all our desires and beyond.

The desires are both worldly and spiritual. Our ultimate goal or desire is to attain the Moksha (मोक्ष).

Tulsidasji here says that Hanumanji has the power to fulfill our desires to a state beyond what we can think of, thereby giving us the ultimate enlightenment and liberation.

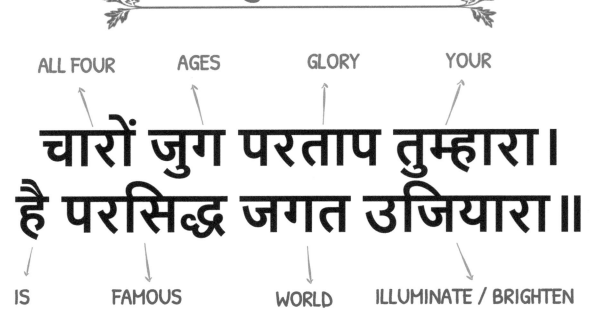

ALL FOUR   AGES   GLORY   YOUR

चारों जुग परताप तुम्हारा।
है परसिद्ध जगत उजियारा॥

IS   FAMOUS   WORLD   ILLUMINATE / BRIGHTEN

charon juga partaap tumhara | hai parsidh jagat ujiyara ||

Your glory is famous across times and ages (all four ages)
And your glory illuminates the whole world

There are four Yuga (युग) or Ages.
Satya Yuga – Age of Truth (सत्य). This is considered the most perfect and best time. There was complete honesty and virtue in this time and everyone lived peacefully.
Treta Yuga – The second Yuga where the virtue slightly diminishes. This age is still considered very good and was the age of Sri Ram. Here although Treta means third, it actually denotes only three quarters of virtue.

Dwapar Yuga – This is the third Yuga. In thi age, virtue further diminishes but there is sti the balance of good and bad. This was the ag of Sri Krishna. Dwapar means two and signifie only two quarters of virtue left.
Kali Yuga – The final and current age. This is th age of gradual decay of all virtues. It is believe that when the world will descend into complet chaos, Vishnu will incarnate as Kalki in his tent avatar to end the world and start again.

SAGES SAINTS YOU PROTECTOR

साधु संत के तुम रखवारे।
असुर निकंदन राम दुलारे॥

DEMONS DESTROYER SRI RAM DEAR

sadhu sant ke tum rakhvare। asura nikandan ram dulare॥

You are the protector of Sadhu (sages) and Sants (saints)
You are the destroyer of demons and you are very dear to Sri Ram

When Hanumanji flew to Lanka to look for Mata Sita, he met many demons on the way. He killed or overcame all of them to complete his mission. He first encountered Surasa who wanted to eat Hanumanji. Hanumanji expanded his size and so did Surasa by expanding her mouth. All of a sudden Hanuman took a tiny form entered her mouth and exited from her ear.

Next, he met Simhika. She constantly ate Hanumanji's shadow and Hanumanji fell down. Then Hanumanji enters her mouth and using his sharp fingers tore her tummy and came out.
Finally, at the gates of Lanka, he met Lankini who was the protector Goddess of Lanka. Hanumanji and Lankini had a fight and she let Hanumanji enter Lanka.
Therefore Hanumanji is also called the destroyer of demons (असुर निकंदन).

EIGHT — QUALITIES/DIVINE POWERS — NINE — TREASURE — OF — GIVER

अष्ट सिद्धि नौ निधि के दाता।
अस बर दीन्ह जानकी माता॥

THIS — BOON — GAVE — DAUGHTER OF JANAK SITA — MOTHER

astha siddhi nau nidhi ke data | asa bar dinha janaki mata ||

You are the giver of eight divine powers and nine treasures
This was the boon given by Mata Sita so you can bless your devotees with these powers

There are eight qualities of perfection (सिद्धि) and nine treasures (निधि) as per our scriptures. Hanumanji has received these as a boon (वरदान) from Gods.

Mata Sita gave the boon to Hanumanji that whoever prays to him, Hanumanji can bless his devotees who these eight qualities and nine treasures.

Mata Sita is also referred to as Janaki (जानकी) as she was daughter of King Janak who ruled Mithila at that time.

The present day region around Nepal and Bihar is believed to be the ancient kingdom of Mithila.

This is where King Janak found Sita when he was ploughing a field. Sita is thus also called the daughter of Mother Earth (भूमि देवी)

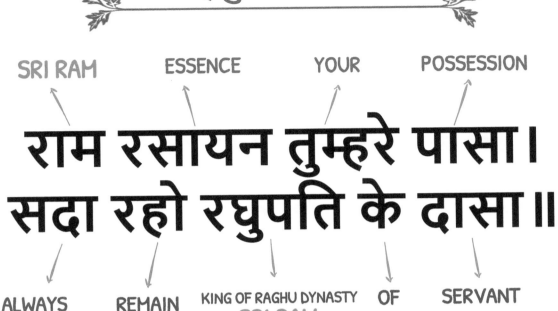

ram rasayana tumhare pasa| sada raho raghupati ke dasa‖

You possess/have the magical essence of devotion to Sri Ram
Always remain as the servant/devotee of Raghupati (Sri Ram)

The more common English meaning of Rasayana (रसायन) is chemical. Here Rasayana is also a Sanskrit word meaning path (ayana) of essence (rasa).

Tulsidasji refers to devotion and bhakti to Sri Ram as Ram Rasayana. Hanumanji is known as the greatest devotee of Sri Ram.

Valmikiji was earlier born to Brahmin parents. As per legends, he later became a bandit and once tried to rob Sapta Rishis. They asked him to chant the name of Ram. He was unable to utter Ram (राम) and kept chanting Mara (मरा). Mara means dead.

In course of time chanting of Mara turned to Ram and he became Maharishi Valmiki and wrote Ramayana. Such is the power of Ram name (Ram Rasayana).

श्री हनुमान चालीसा

YOUR   DEVOTIONAL SONG   SRI RAM   GETS

तुम्हरे भजन राम को पावै।
जनम जनम के दुख बिसरावै॥

LIFE   LIFE   SORROWS   FREE OF
MULTIPLE BIRTHS

tumhare bhajan ram ko pave | janam janam ke dukh bisrave ||

Singing your bhajan (song) gets Sri Ram
And we can be free of sorrows of many births

Bhajans (भजन) are very important part of our culture. It is derived from the Sanskrit word bhaj meaning to revere and respect.

Bhajans are melodious songs written and sung in the glory of Lord. The sweet melody of any bhajan evokes special energy within us creating a lot of positivity.

In our culture, we believe in the constant cycle of life, death and rebirth. Each birth gives us an opportunity to evolve as better humans based on our actions or karma (कर्म). The ultimate goal of human life is to attain moksha (मोक्ष) and free us from this cycle of life and death.

Tulsidasji here says singing the glory of Hanumanji helps us get to Sri Ram and frees us from the sorrows of many lifetimes.

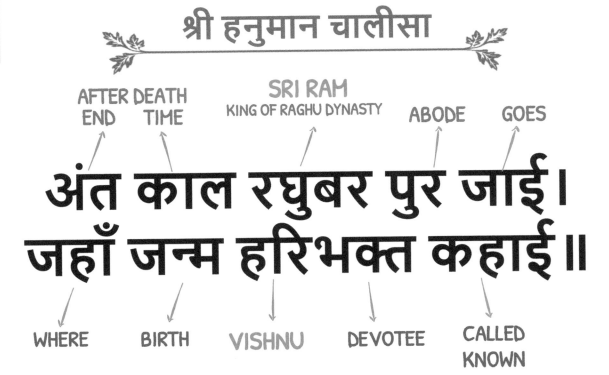

anta kaal raghubar pur jaayee | jahan janam hari bhakta kahai ||

At the end after death one goes to Sri Ram's (Raghubar) abode
And whenever he takes a new birth he is known as a devotee of Lord
Sri Ram

Hanumanji is said to be immortal. As a child, he was blessed immortality by Brahma after he was struck by Indra's Vajra. Sri Ram also blessed Hanumanji with a very long life.

As per some belief, Hanumanji is still guarding the earth and waiting for Vishnu to appear in his tenth and last avatar as Kalki.

Tulsidasji says to Hanumanji that in the end, he will go to the abode of Lord Vishnu at Vaikuntha. And after that, he will always be known as a devotee of Sri Ram.

Another meaning of the line is that if we pray to Hanumanji we all can enter the abode of Sri Ram and on each birth, we will be known as Hari Bhakt (हरि भक्त).

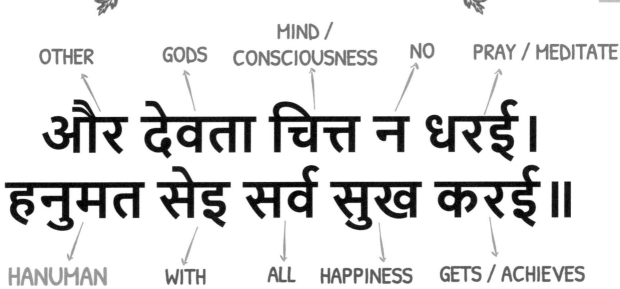

OTHER GODS MIND / CONSCIOUSNESS NO PRAY / MEDITATE

और देवता चित्त न धरई।
हनुमत सेइ सर्व सुख करई॥

HANUMAN WITH ALL HAPPINESS GETS / ACHIEVES

aur devta chitta na dharaee | hanumat sei sarva sukha karaee ||

Even if we do not meditate on any other Gods
We can still get all kinds of happiness by praying to Hanumanji alone

These are some of the great verses by Tulsidasji. In this line, Tulsidasji tells us the importance of a devotee to the Lord. A true devotee is revered more than Lord.

Hanumanji was one of the greatest devotees of Sri Ram. Thus, even if we do not pray to all other Gods and pray to Hanumanji, we can still get all the happiness in life.

As a kid, Hanumanji devoured Sun thinking of it as a red fruit. This descended the whole world into darkness. Indra was really angry on this child and strikes him with his vajra, thereby disfiguring his jaw.

The meaning of Hanuman is one who has a disfigured jaw.

sankat kate mite sab peera | jo sumire hanumat balbeera ||

Difficulties disappear and all pain are relieved
To those who remembers the mighty Hanumat (Hanuman)

Tulsidasji in this line, emphasises on one of the most appealing images of Hanumanji, the reliever of all difficulties. In Ramayana, Hanumanji has solved problems for Sri Ram on multiple occasions. So, if we pray to him with our pure heart, he will free us of all difficulties and pain.

Hanumanji has been shown as one of the most versatile and resourceful devotees of Sri Ram.
There are different characteristics of Hanumanji. He is an embodiment of selfless devotion. In some scenes, he is shown to be extremely loving or a symbol of dedication and perseverance.
In this line, he is shown as someone with strength and valour (बलबीरा).

VICTORY / VICTORIOUS   HANUMAN   MASTER OF ALL SENSES

जय जय जय हनुमान गोसाईं।
कृपा करहु गुरुदेव की नाईं॥

GRACE   DO / SHOWER   TEACHER SUPREME GURU   GOD   LIKE

jai jai jai hanuman gosai| kripa karahu gurudev ki naai||

Victory to you O Master of Senses
Please shower your grace me like the Supreme Guru

Hanumanji has been referred to as Goswami or Gosai in this line, meaning who has control over all his senses. In order to be victorious in all walks of life, one needs to be in control of all their senses and emotions. And there is no perfect example than Hanumanji who is always so down to earth and selfless in all his actions and achievements.

In our culture, a Teacher or Guru (गुरु) has always been given the utmost importance Kabir Dasji once wrote this in the glory of Guru

गुरु गोविन्द दोऊ खड़े काके लागूं पांय।
बलिहारी गुरु अपने गोविन्द दियो बताय॥

Meaning if both Guru and Lord are standing in front of me whom should I bow. Lord himsel directs us to bow to our Guru first.

श्री हनुमान चालीसा

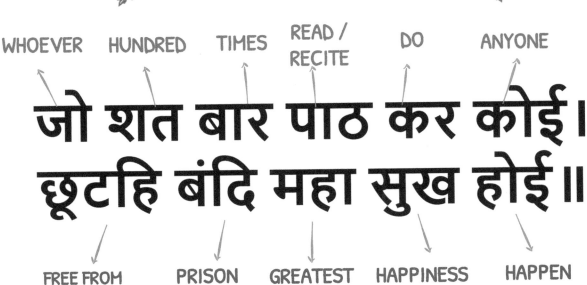

WHOEVER HUNDRED TIMES READ / RECITE DO ANYONE

जो शत बार पाठ कर कोई।
छूटहि बंदि महा सुख होई॥

FREE FROM PRISON GREATEST HAPPINESS HAPPEN

jo shat baar path kar koi| chutahi bandi maha sukha hoi||

Whoever chants the Hanuman Chalisa for hundred times
Is freed from all kinds of bondages and obtains the greatest happiness

Although, Tulsidasji in this line says that whoever reads the Hanuman Chalisa a hundred times, hundred can also be interpreted as just a number here. The essence is to keep repeating Hanuman Chalisa and try and imbibe the qualities of Hanumanji in our life as much as possible.

Repeating Hanuman Chalisa a hundred times or any number of times with true heart frees us from all kinds of worldly bondages and the cycle of life and death. We are truly liberated with the blessings of Hanumanji and get the ultimate bliss.

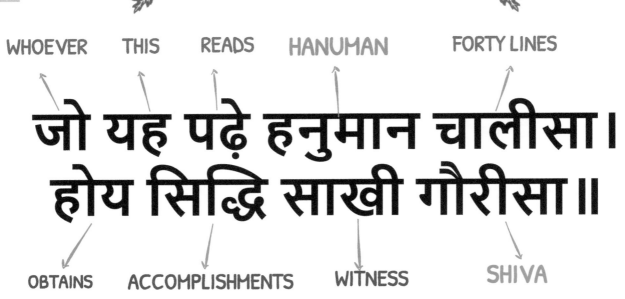

WHOEVER · THIS · READS · HANUMAN · FORTY LINES

जो यह पढ़े हनुमान चालीसा।
होय सिद्धि साखी गौरीसा॥

OBTAINS · ACCOMPLISHMENTS · WITNESS · SHIVA

jo yah padhe hanuman chalisa | hoye siddhi saakhi gaurisa ||

Whoever reads this Hanuman Chalisa
Gets all kinds of accomplishments in life and Shiva is witness to this

In Hinduism, Brahma, Vishnu and Shiva are the Trinity Gods. Brahma is the creator, Vishnu the preserver and Shiva is the destroyer. When the world comes to a stage where it becomes difficult to live, then Shiva destroys the world so that it can be created again by Brahma. This is a cosmic cycle that keeps the world going.

Shiva is also called Mahadev or the Greatest God.

Tuslidasji here invokes Shiva and says that if we read the Hanuman Chalisa regularly then we can get all accomplishments in life and if Shiva is witness to this, then there is no reason for doubt.

Hanumanji is believed to be an incarnation of Shiva.

श्री हनुमान चालीसा

TULSIDAS ALWAYS LORD DEVOTEE

तुलसीदास सदा हरि चेरा। कीजै नाथ हृदय महँ डेरा॥

MAKE LORD HEART MY HOME

tulasidas sada hari chera| kijai nath hriday maha dera||

Tulsidas is always a devotee of Hari (Sri Ram)
O Lord (Sri Ram), please make my heart your home. Please reside in my heart

Tulsidasji in this line says that he wishes to be a devotee of Sri Ram forever.

Tulsidasji is considered one of the greatest Indian poets and he dedicated his life to writing several books and poems on Sri Ram and Hanumanji. Tulsidasji spent most of his life on the banks of River Ganga in the holy city of Kashi (now known as Varanasi or Banaras). There is also a ghat named after him in Varanasi called Tulsi Ghat.

Many believe Tulsidasji as reincarnation of Valmiki. Hanumanji went to live in the Himalayas after Sri Ram's victory over Ravan. There, he wrote Sri Ram's story on rocks with his nails. When Valmiki saw this he knew that this can easily overshadow his Ramayana. Hanumanji sensed this and threw his version into the ocean. Valmiki felt really bad and blessed him that he (Valmiki) would be born again and will tell the story of Sri Ram in a different version.

श्री हनुमान चालीसा

पवनतनय संकट हरन मंगल मूरति रूप।
राम लखन सीता सहित हृदय बसहु सुरभूप॥

pavan-tanay sankat haran mangal murati roop |
ram lakhan sita sahit hriday basahu sura bhoop ||

O Son of Vayu, remover of difficulties, one who has auspicious form
The king among Gods (Hanuman) please stay in my heart forever with
Sri Ram, Lakshman and Sita

Tulsidasji says Hanumanji has auspicious (मंगल) form (मूरति). Praying him gives us all kinds of goodness. Mangal also means planet Mars or Mangal grah (मंगल ग्रह).

A lot of people pray to Hanumanji on Tuesday (मंगलवार) and also keep fast on this day as Tuesday is considered to be the day of Hanumanji.

Ganeshji is also called Mangal Murati (मंगल मूरति) like Hanumanji.

Hanumanji is very closely related to Ganpati. Hanumanji is considered an avatar of Shiva while Ganeshji is the son of Shiva.

पवन सुत हनुमान की जय

Victory to Hanuman, Son of Vayu

हनुमान चालीसा

Hanuman Chalisa

श्री गुरु चरन सरोज रज, निज मन मुकुर सुधारि।
बरनौ रघुवर बिमल जसु, जो दायकु फल चारि॥
बुद्धिहीन तनु जानिके, सुमिरौ पवनकुमार।
बल बुद्धि विद्या देहु मोहि हरहु कलेस विकार॥

जय हनुमान ज्ञान गुन सागर। जय कपीस तिहुँ लोक उजागर॥ 1 ॥
राम दूत अतुलित बल धामा। अंजनि पुत्र पवनसुत नामा॥ 2 ॥
महावीर विक्रम बजरंगी। कुमति निवार सुमति के संगी॥ 3 ॥
कंचन बरन बिराज सुबेसा। कानन कुंडल कुंचित केसा॥ 4 ॥
हाथ बज्र औ ध्वजा बिराजै। काँधे मूँज जनेऊ साजै॥ 5 ॥

शंकर सुवन केसरी नंदन। तेज प्रताप महा जग बंदन॥ 6 ॥
विद्यावान गुनी अति चातुर। राम काज करिबे को आतुर॥ 7 ॥
प्रभु चरित्र सुनिबे को रसिया। राम लखन सीता मन बसिया॥ 8 ॥
सूक्ष्म रूप धरी सियहिं दिखावा। बिकट रूप धरि लंक जरावा॥ 9 ॥
भीम रूप धरि असुर सँहारे। रामचन्द्र के काज सँवारे॥ 10 ॥

shree guru charan saroj raj nij man mukur sudhari |
barnou raghuvar bimal jasu jo dayak phal chari || budhhi heen tanu
janike sumiro pavankumar |
bal budhi vidya dehu mohi harhu kalesh vikar ||

jai hanuman gyan gun sagar | jai kapeesh tihu lok ujaagar || 1 ||
ram doot atulit bal dhama | anjani putra pavansut nama || 2 ||
mahaveer vikram bajrangi | kumati niwar sumati ke sangi || 3 ||
kanchan baran beeraj subesha | kaanan kundal kunchit kesa || 4 ||
haath bajra au dhwaja beeraje | kaandhe moonj janeu saaje || 5 ||

shankar suvan kesari nandan | tej pratap maha jag bandan || 6
vidyavaan gunee ati chaatur | ram kaaj karibe ko aatur || 7 ||
prabhu charitra sunibe ko rasiya | ram lakhan sita man basiya || 8 ||
sukshma roop dharee siyahi dikhava | bikat roop dhari lanka jarava || 9 ||
bhima roop dhari asura sanhare | ramchandra ke kaaj sanware || 10 ||

लाय सँजीवनि लखन जियाए। श्रीरघुबीर हरषि उर लाए॥ 11 ॥
रघुपति कीन्हीं बहुत बड़ाई। तुम मम प्रिय भरतहि सम भाई॥ 12 ॥
सहस बदन तुम्हरो जस गावैं। अस कहि श्रीपति कंठ लगावैं॥ 13 ॥
सनकादिक ब्रह्मादि मुनीसा। नारद सारद सहित अहीसा॥ 14 ॥
जम कुबेर दिक्पाल जहाँ ते। कबी कोबिद कहि सकैं कहाँ ते॥ 15 ॥

तुम उपकार सुग्रीवहिं कीन्हा। राम मिलाय राजपद दीन्हा॥ 16 ॥
तुम्हरो मन्त्र बिभीषन माना। लंकेश्वर भए सब जग जाना॥ 17 ॥
जुग सहस्र जोजन पर भानू। लील्यो ताहि मधुर फल जानू॥ 18 ॥
प्रभु मुद्रिका मेलि मुख माहीं। जलधि लाँघि गये अचरज नाहीं॥ 19 ॥
दुर्गम काज जगत के जेते । सुगम अनुग्रह तुम्हरे तेते॥ 20 ॥

राम दुआरे तुम रखवारे। होत न आज्ञा बिनु पैसारे॥ 21 ॥
सब सुख लहै तुम्हारी शरना। तुम रक्षक काहू को डरना॥ 22 ॥
आपन तेज सम्हारो आपै। तीनौं लोक हाँक ते काँपे॥ 23 ॥
भूत पिशाच निकट नहिं आवै। महाबीर जब नाम सुनावै॥ 24 ॥
नासै रोग हरै सब पीरा। जपत निरंतर हनुमत बीरा॥ 25 ॥

laye sanjeevani lakhan jiyaye | shree raghubeer harshi ur laaye || 11 ||
raghupati keenhee bahut bada | tum mum priya bharathi sama bhai || 12 ||
sahas badan tumharo jas gaaven | as kahi shreepati kanth lagaaven || 13 ||
sanaka-adik brahmadi munisa | naarad shaarad sahi ahisa || 14 ||
jam kuber dikpal jahaan te | kabi kobid kahi saken kahaan te || 15 ||

tum upkaar sugrivahin keenha | ram milaay rajpad deenha || 16 ||
tumharo mantra vibhishan mana | lankeshwar bhaye sab jag jaana || 17 ||
juga sahastra jojan par bhaanu | lilyo taahi madhur phal jaanoo || 18 ||
prabhu mudrika meli much maaheen | jaladhi laanghi gaye acharaj
naahi || 19 ||
durgam kaaj jagat ke jete | sugam anugrah tumhare tete || 20 ||

ram duare tum rakhvaare | hota na aagya binu paisaare || 21 ||
sab sukh lahe tumhari sharna | tum rakshak kaahu ko darna || 22 ||
aapan tej samharo aape | teeno lok haank te kaanpe || 23 ||
bhoot pisaach nikat nahi aavei | mahaveer jab naam sunaave || 24 ||
nase rog hare sab peera | japat nirantar hanumat veera || 25 ||

संकट तें हनुमान छुड़ावै। मन क्रम बचन ध्यान जो लावै॥ 26 ॥
सब पर राम तपस्वी राजा। तिन के काज सकल तुम साजा॥ 27 ॥
और मनोरथ जो कोई लावै। सोहि अमित जीवन फल पावै॥ 28 ॥
चारों जुग परताप तुम्हारा। है परसिद्ध जगत उजियारा॥ 29 ॥
साधु संत के तुम रखवारे। असुर निकंदन राम दुलारे॥ 30 ॥

अष्ट सिद्धि नौ निधि के दाता। अस बर दीन्ह जानकी माता॥ 31 ॥
राम रसायन तुम्हरे पासा। सदा रहो रघुपति के दासा॥ 32 ॥
तुम्हरे भजन राम को पावै। जनम जनम के दुख बिसरावै॥ 33 ॥
अंत काल रघुबर पुर जाई। जहाँ जन्म हरिभक्त कहाई॥ 34 ॥
और देवता चित्त न धरई। हनुमत सेइ सर्व सुख करई॥ 35 ॥

संकट कटै मिटै सब पीरा। जो सुमिरै हनुमत बलबीरा॥ 36 ॥
जय जय जय हनुमान गोसाईं। कृपा करहु गुरुदेव की नाईं॥ 37 ॥
जो शत बार पाठ कर कोई। छूटहि बंदि महा सुख होई॥ 38 ॥
जो यह पढ़े हनुमान चालीसा। होय सिद्धि साखी गौरीसा॥ 39 ॥
तुलसीदास सदा हरि चेरा। कीजै नाथ हृदय महँ डेरा॥ 40 ॥

पवनतनय संकट हरन मंगल मूरति रूप।
राम लखन सीता सहित हृदय बसहु सुर भूप॥

sankat te hanuman churave | man kram bachan dhyan jo laave || 26 ||
sab par ram tapasvee raja | tin ke kaaj sakal tum saja || 27 ||
aur manorath jo koi laave | sohi amit jeevan phal pave || 28 ||
charon juga partaap tumhara | hai parsidh jagat ujiyara || 29 ||
sadhu sant ke tum rakhvare | asura nikandan ram dulare || 30 ||

astha siddhi nau nidhi ke data | asa bar dinha janaki mata || 31 ||
ram rasayana tumhare pasa | sada raho raghupati ke dasa || 32 ||
tumhare bhajan ram ko pave | janam janam ke dukh bisrave || 33 ||
anta kaal raghubar pur jaayee | jahan janam hari bhakta kahai || 34 ||
aur devta chitta na dharaee | hanumat sei sarva sukha karaee || 35 ||

sankat kate mite sab peera | jo sumire hanumat balbeera || 36 ||
jai jai jai hanuman gosai | kripa karahu gurudev ki naai || 37 ||
jo shat baar path kar koi | chutahi bandi maha sukha hoi || 38 ||
jo yah padhe hanuman chalisa | hoye siddhi saakhi gaurisa || 39 ||
tulasidas sada hari chera | kijai nath hriday maha dera || 40 ||

pavan-tanay sankat haran mangal murati roop |
ram lakhan sita sahit hriday basahu sura bhoop ||

Trivia
and
Short Stories

Was Hanumanji a Monkey or Vanara?

One of the most common representation of Hanumanji in popular art and culture is that of a monkey. But was Hanumanji a monkey or vanara?

If you look at the word Vanara, it comprises of two common Sanskrit words: Vana + Nara (वन + नर). Vana means forest and Nara means man, therefore literally meaning one who lives in the forest or forest dwellers. As per Valimiki Ramayana vanaras were vanacharina (वनचारिणा) meaning people who roamed around in forest.

Another very common misconception is that people who lived in the forest are not intelligent compared to the city dwellers. This image ties nicely with the image of a monkey as tree hopping unintelligent creature. However, we cannot be more incorrect in our understanding on this.

In the very first line of Hanuman Chalisa, Tulsidasji calls Hanumanji ocean of knowledge and wisdom (ज्ञान गुन सागर). Hanumanji was one of the most intelligent and erudite Vanara of his time who had knowledge of all four vedas was an expert in grammar. In the Kishkindha kanda, Valmikiji refers to Hanumanji as the most ablest sentence maker (वाक्य कोविदः 4-2-13) and (महानुभावो 4-2-29) the most marvellous one. When Sugriva asks Hanumanji to go and meet Ram and Lakshman who were coming towards Mount Rishyamuka in search of Mata Sita, he requests him to go and meet them in his natural form (त्वया प्राकृतेन एव गत्वा 4-2-24). Hanumanji then goes to meet Sri Ram as a sage in human form and not in his monkey form.

Thus from all the details above it should be more than evident that Hanumanji and all the Vanaras were not monkeys but highly accomplished human beings living in forests. In most likelihood they used to wear masks and tails like many tribal cultures thereby resembling as monkeys. The word vanara may have slowly changed to monkey in subsequent retellings and translations.

Hanumanji's birth name is not known. The name Hanuman in Sanskrit means someone with a disfigured jaw. When Hanumanji was a child, he leapt into the sky to reach for Sun thinking of it as a sweet fruit. All Gods were really scared and they requested Devraj Indra for help. Indra struck Bal Hanuman with his Vajra (thunderbolt) and Hanuman fell on the ground disfiguring his mouth and thereby got the name **Hanuman**.

Hanumanji's parent's names were Anjana and Kesari. Anjana was an apsara and was born on earth after a curse from Sage Durvasa while Kesari was a vanara chief.

Hanumanji is Lord Shiva's avatar. Anjana and Kesari prayed to Mahadeva for a child and were blessed with a son. Shiva instructed Vayu, the Wind God to carry his divine powers to Anjana and thus Hanumanji was born.

Hanumanji is known as son of Vayu, the God of Wind/Air and is known by many names of Vayu.

Vayu (वायु) – Vayu-putra
Pavan (पवन) – Pavan-putra, Pavan-suta, Pavan-tanay
Marut (मारुत) - Maruti, Maruti-nandan

Tulsidasji was born in 1497 and lived for almost 125 years singing and writing the glories of Sri Ram, Sri Krishna and Hanumanji. He spent most of his life in Varanasi on the banks of River Ganga. He is said to be one of the greatest Hindi poets. He wrote several works including the famous Awadhi version of Ramayana called Ramacharitmanas. He is also credited to writing Hanuman Chalisa, the forty verses in the praise of Hanumanji. His other famous works include Hanuman Ashtak (eight verses of Hanumanji).

It is widely believed that Hanumanji gave darshan to Tulsidasji. This is also hinted in some of his literary works. There is also the Sankat Mochan Hanuman Temple in Varanasi where Tulsidasji is believed to have met Hanumanji.

Hanuman Chalisa is a compilation of 43 verses. Although Chalis (चालीसा) means forty in Hindi there are more than forty verses in Hanuman Chalisa. The text is composed of 2 Dohas at the beginning followed by 40 Choupais and ending with 1 Doha at the end.

In Hanuman Chalisa, Tulsidasji has addressed Hanumanji, Sri Ram and Mata Sita by their multiple names.
Hanuman – Pavankumar, Bajrangi, Mahaveer, Kesari Nandan, Shankar Suvan, Hanumat, Pavantanay
Ram – Raghuvar, Prabhu, Ramchandra, Raghubeer, Raghupati, Shreepati
Sita – Siyahi, Janaki

Hanuman's Ramayana

Hanumanji is also credited with writing with his own version of Ramayana. After Sri Ram's victory over Ravan, Hanumanji went on to live in the mountains of Himalaya. There he started writing the glories of Sri Ram using only his nails on the mountain rocks. Rishi Valmiki was also writing the story of Sri Ram, the original Ramayana. When he came to know about it, he went to see Hanumanji and requested him to show his version. Hanumanji carried him on his shoulder and placed him on the mountain where he could read this. Valmikiji was very impressed with this and said there cannot be any other story even close to this. Hanumanji did not want to diminish Valmikiji's glory and immediately drowned his version into the ocean. Valmikiji then blessed Hanumanji and said he will take birth again and will devote his life singing his praise. He also said he will retell the story using the language of common man.

Therefore, Tulsidasji is believed to be the reincarnation of Rishi Valmiki. Tulsidasji spent his life writing the glories of Hanumanji and Sri Ram. He wrote his version of Ramayan in Awadhi language, a dialect of Hindi spoken around Ayodhya called Ramcharitmanas. Tulsidasji's Ramcharitmanas is still the most popular version of Ramayan today.

There are multiple versions of Ramayana across India and South-East Asia. Each version has it's own storyline and interpretation with Sri Ram being the central character. The oldest Ramayana is said to be authored by Narada Rishi called Mula Ramayana. The earliest known version available to us in Sanskrit is the Valmiki Ramayana. And the most common version read across India is Ramcharitmanas penned by Tulsidasji.

Sri Ram in Hanumanji's heart

Sri Ram returned to Ayodhya after 14 years of exile and victory over Ravan and was crowned the King of Ayodhya. He wanted to thank every one and gave them various gifts and presents. He asked Mata Sita to give a gift to Hanumanji. She gifted Hanumanji a necklace of pearls.

Hanumanji analyzed the necklace minutely and started to bit every pearl of the necklace and throw them away. Everybody was amused by Hanumanji's behaviour and asked him why is he throwing away the pearls. Hanumanji replied that he could not find Sri Ram in any of the pearls and therefore they are of no value to him. Vibhishan then asks Hanumanji what about Hanumanji himself. Does he have Sri Ram in it or even he is worthless. Hanumanji immediately tore his chest with his nails and everyone was amazed to see the reflection of Sri Ram and Mata Sita in it.

Hanumanji covered in Sindoor

Once Hanumanji saw Mata Sita apply red sindoor (vermillion) on her forehead. He was very intrigued and asked her about it. Not knowing how to explain the meaning of it, she said that the red dot represented her love for Sri Ram and was also for the long life of Prabhu Sri Ram. He got really excited hearing this and immediately went out and covered his entire body with red vermillion. When Mata Sita saw this, she was really amused and asked him why did he cover his body in red color. He then explained if a small red dot can bring long life then he applied the same over his entire body for Sri Ram's longer life and to show his love for his master.

Bhima meets Hanuman

During Mahabharata once Draupadi asked Bhima to look for Saugandhika flower. While searching for the flower, Bhima came across an old monkey lying in his path with his tail stretched out. Bhima arrogantly asked the monkey to move his tail. The monkey said as he is really old, Bhima can do it himself. At this, Bhima got really angry and tried to lift the tail with his left hand and wanted to swing it in the air. To his surprise, he was not able to move the tail at all. He quickly realized that this was no ordinary monkey and immediately asked for his forgiveness. The monkey then revealed himself to be Hanumanji, his brother as both were son of Vayu. He forgave Bhima and blessed him with additional strength.

Makardhwaj – Hanuman's son

Although Hanumanji was a Brahmachari (celibate), he had a son name Makardhwaj. As per one legend after burning the golden city of Lanka, Hanumanji was very sweaty and tired. He took a dip into the ocean and a drop of his sweat fell into the mouth of a giant fish named Makara. Later, Makar was caught by Ahiravan and a half vanara half makar child was discovered from its stomach. Because of this child's power and strength, Ahiravan gave Makardhwaj the task of guarding Paataal, his kingdown.
Later, during the war of Ramayana, Ahiravan captured Ram and Lakshman and took them to Paataal. Hanumanji came to their rescue and met with brave Makardhwaj on the gates of Paataal. He ultimately fights and defeats Makardhwaj and also kills Ahiravan. Hanumanji rescues Ram and Lakshman from Paataal and blessed Makardhwaj. Sri Ram declares Makardhwaj as the king of Paataal loka.

Asura Nikandan (असुर निकंदन) – Demon Slayer

Surasa

During his flight to Lanka, a mountain appears on his way and asks Hanumanji to take some rest. Determined not to lose his focus Hanumanji refuses to rest and moves along. Just then a rakshasi, Surasa, appears and tries to eat Hanuman. She says the only way to move forward is through her mouth. She expands her mouth to the size of mountain. Hanumanji doubles his size as well. This went on for some time and all of a sudden Hanumanji assumes a tiny form and enters and exits her mouth. Surasa then explains that she was sent by Gods to test his abilities and blesses on his endeavour to find Sita.

Simhika

Next, he comes across another rakshasi, Simhika, who used to catch shadows of any creature flying above leading them to fall in the sea and eat them. She tried to do the same with Haunamaji. Hanumanji instantly understood her deceit and enters Simhika's mouth. He uses his sharp nails to tear her stomach and comes out killing the demoness.

Lankini

After reaching Lanka, he climbs up a mountain and sees a large fort surrounded by sea and walls glittering with gold. He also sees demons guarding the fort on all direction. Hanumanji takes a tiny form and tries to enter Lanka. There he encounters Lankini, the protector of Lanka. She interrogates Hanumanji and stops him from entering Lanka. Hanumanji determined not to be stopped at any cost punches her. She falls on the ground and realises that he is no ordinary being. Lankini asks his forgiveness. She also reveals this event as Lord Brahma's prophecy and that Ravan's time is over now.

Giver of Eight Sidhhi and Nine Nidhi (अष्ट सिद्धि नौ निधि के दाता)

The Eight Sidhhi (सिद्धि) and Nine Nidhi (निधि) mentioned in Hanuman Chalisa are as follows:

Eight Sidhhi (Divine Powers)

1. Aṇimā (अणिमा)   : Ability to reduce one's size
2. Mahima (महिमा)   : Ability to increase one's size
3. Garima (गरिमा)   : Ability to increase one's weight infinitely
4. Laghima (लघिमा)   : Ability to become lighter than the lightest
5. Prāpti (प्राप्ति)   : Ability to obtain anything
6. Prākāmya (प्राकम्या)   : Ability to acquire anything desired
7. Iṣiṭva (ईशत्व)   : Ability to have absolute lordship
8. Vaśtva (वस्तव)   : Ability to have control over things

Nine Nidhi (Treasures)

1. Mahapadma (महापद्म) : Greatest Lotus Flower
2. Padma (पद्म)   : Lotus Flower
3. Shankha (शंख)   : Conch
4. Makar (मकर)   : Crocodile
5. Kachhapa (कच्छप)   : Tortoise
6. Mukund (मुकुंद)   : Precious Stone
7. Kunda (कुंद)   : Jasmine
8. Neel (नील)   : Sapphire
9. Kharva (खर्व)   : Dwarf

Kubera, the god of wealth, is the custodian of these nidhis. The nidhis are very mystical. Though the references to it are present in our ancient texts, it has still not been understood completely and many experts offer their own interpretation.

Hanumanji had all eight sidhhi and demonstrated them on several occasions in Ramayana. He was also blessed by Mata Sita as a giver of these to the devotees.

Rahul Agrawal is a Information Technology Consultant by profession. He has two kids aged 6 and 1 and lives in Melbourne, Australia. Rahul has a very keen interest in the magnificent history of India and likes to read books on ancient India. He has been narrating a lot of these stories to his 6 year old son. Once while explaining the meaning of Hanuman Chalisa to his son, the idea of making Hanuman Chalisa simple and easy for kids originated and together they started the "Hanuman Chalisa Project".

Follow Rahul on Twitter  @rahulwritesin

Connect with us on

  @hanumanchalisabook

Thanks a lot for buying this book and trying to connect your child with glories of Sri Ramchandraji and Hanumanji. We would love your feedback about the book. Please connect with us using any of the above channels. Let us know how your child is learning Hanuman Chalisa and benefiting from it. Please send us a picture if you can of your child reading the book. Jai Sri Ram.
- Rahul Agrawal

Lightning Source UK Ltd.
Milton Keynes UK
UKHW051840260321
381040UK00002B/48

9 789354 080180